Performance Reviews

Get up to speed fast on essential business skills. Whether you're looking for a crash course or a brief refresher, you'll find just what you need in HBR's 20-Minute Manager series—foundational reading for ambitious professionals and aspiring executives. Each book is a concise, practical primer, so you'll have time to brush up on a variety of key management topics.

Advice you can quickly read and apply, from the most trusted source in business.

Titles include:

Creating Business Plans

Delegating Work

Finance Basics

Innovative Teams

Getting Work Done

Giving Effective Feedback

Managing Projects

Managing Time

Managing Up

Performance Reviews

Presentations

Running Meetings

20 MINUTE MANAGER SERIES

Performance Reviews

Evaluate performance
Offer constructive feedback
Discuss tough topics

HARVARD BUSINESS REVIEW PRESS

Boston, Massachusetts

Copyright 2015 Harvard Business School Publishing Corporation

Library of Congress Cataloging-in-Publication Data
Performance reviews : prepare for the meeting, offer constructive feedback, discuss tough topics.
    pages cm. — (20 minute manager series)
    Includes index.
    ISBN 978-1-63369-006-6 1. Employees—Rating of.
    2. Employees—Evaluation.   3. Performance standards.
I. Harvard Business Review Press.
    HF5549.5.R3P478 2015
    658.3'125—dc23

                                        2014041167

ISBN: 9781633690066
eISBN: 9781633690073

Preview

You've just received word that it's time to conduct annual performance reviews for your direct reports. You know these evaluations offer a great opportunity for change and growth—for stellar employees, subpar performers, and those in between. But year after year, you find yourself ill prepared, and your assessment ends up being more of a formality than an opportunity for employee improvement. This book walks you through the step-by-step process of conducting performance reviews so you'll be better equipped when it comes time for this crucial task. You'll learn to:

- Use direct observation and other resources to make an objective assessment

- Formally document your evaluation

- Discuss both achievements and performance gaps

- Turn negative feedback into a productive conversation

- Set challenging but achievable goals

- Make feedback and follow-up an ongoing part of your job

Contents

Contents

Performance Reviews

The Basics

The Basics

E very year you're faced with the same task: You must conduct performance reviews with your direct reports. When handled correctly, this process can result in better job performance and higher morale within your team, which can have a positive influence on your entire organization.

But reviewing and assessing a person's performance, not to mention discussing your evaluation with that individual, can be demanding and stressful. This is your opportunity to help your employees improve, but like most managers, you probably don't enjoy telling people they're not performing as well as they could or should. It's particularly challenging to broach the topic of constructive feedback with an employee whose overall performance is less than satisfactory. And even a review of a high-achiever requires careful preparation, documentation, and follow-up to be effective.

This book will teach you the basics of conducting performance reviews, from evaluating an employee's performance and documenting your assessment to having the conversation, recording what happened, and following up. The advice in this book will also help you grow more comfortable with the performance review process by giving you techniques for tackling those tough conversations. Finally, you'll learn how to make evaluating performance and giving feedback a regular part of your job throughout the year, so that when review time rolls around again, you're not left stressed and scrambling.

What is a performance review?

A performance review is the process of evaluating the quality of your employees' work and discussing your assessment with them. It is usually conducted annually, with follow-ups as needed. These formal appraisals are an important part of performance management—which includes activities such as goal setting, regular feedback, review, and employee development—and is used to measure and improve employee effectiveness on an ongoing basis.

Just like a doctor conducting a yearly physical, an annual review affords you the opportunity to identify what's going well with an employee's performance and to diagnose problems before they worsen. For the recipient of the review, it answers two critical questions: *What is expected of me?* and *How well am I meeting those expectations?* Both the recipient and the reviewer then have the chance to discuss opportunities for growth, strategize how to correct course if problems exist, and collaborate on new yearly targets so the employee can move forward in his job and career.

Performance reviews also provide organizations with vital data needed to make and justify staffing decisions by assessing the overall strength of their workforce, identifying top contributors and candidates for promotion, and pinpointing subpar performers. In addition, these evaluations protect your organization with documentation in the case of legal challenges by disgruntled employees who have been terminated, demoted, or denied a raise.

Attentive guidance and coaching, whether scheduled or spontaneous, should be an ongoing part of your working relationship throughout the year (and, in fact, are pivotal to having an accurate depiction of your direct report's performance when review time comes around again). But a formal annual review reinforces that effort by giving you a predetermined opportunity to share feedback with your employees and to officially record that feedback for the organization and for future reference.

The performance review process

Your organization's HR department may already have an established performance review system that you should follow or a formal evaluation form you need to complete. If so, be aware of those requirements, and shift your implementation of the process outlined in this book accordingly. If your organization doesn't have any formal procedures or documentation in place for performance reviews, this book provides a process and tools that you can use. This process includes:

- Evaluating your employee's performance throughout the year

- Documenting your impressions

- Gathering necessary materials, including your employee's self-appraisal and 360-degree feedback

- Finding a suitable time and place for the meeting

- Setting the right tone during the discussion

- Offering feedback that the recipient can use to grow

- Defining next steps, including setting goals and creating a development plan

- Following up with your direct report

- Assessing your effectiveness in the appraisal process

Following these steps will make the performance review process less stressful for you and more useful for your employee.

Involve your employee

While it may seem that the performance review process rests solely on your shoulders, your employee plays his part as well. As a manager, you'll be in charge of the review process and lead the discussion. In advance of your meeting, you'll gather and evaluate information about the employee's performance and write a formal appraisal. In the review meeting itself, you'll discuss your assessment with the employee and engage him in a dialogue to plan improvements.

But an appraisal is not intended to present a one-sided point of view. To make the appraisal as objective and effective as possible, you should involve your employee in the process long before the formal meeting. By conducting regular feedback discussions throughout the year and asking the employee to complete a self-appraisal as the review itself approaches, you will promote trust, establish a tone of partnership and cooperation, prevent surprises, and help temper negative reactions to constructive feedback. Finally, your employee will feel he has contributed to the appraisal, rather than being a passive recipient of your evaluation.

Now that you understand what a performance review entails and how your employee can be involved, let's turn our attention to the evaluation process, which starts with getting the right information.

Gathering Information

Gathering Information

Assessing an employee's performance isn't something you do once, a week before conducting a review discussion—it's an ongoing process. Your information gathering, likewise, should be a part of your daily work throughout the year. To get a complete picture of your employee and fairly evaluate her work, collect information about her performance from a number of different sources.

Observe and track employee progress

Direct observation is the best way to monitor employee performance. It can help you identify strengths and weaknesses and understand the impact those capabilities will have on your employee's ability to achieve specific goals. In a fast-paced workplace, attentive observation is especially important: If an individual is headed off track, you need to know about it early, before problems are compounded. Flagging issues when they first arise will enable you to take corrective action and help your employee get back on course.

Keep notes about your observations throughout the year so you're not relying on memory when it's time to do a formal assessment. It's difficult to remember everything your employee did over the course of the year, and her most recent work is probably what's fresh in your mind. Maybe your employee saved the day in January but made a mammoth mistake in June. When her July review comes around, which event are you more likely to recall?

Consider these two approaches for tracking employee performance:

- Keep a notebook, file, or folder on each of your direct reports handy, and update it regularly with notes on their performance. Set a reminder in your calendar to periodically add entries.

- Request short, informal monthly progress reports from each of your employees. You might specify a few topics to cover, such as key accomplishments, problems, or concerns, and what the individual plans to accomplish in the next month. The quality, completeness, and timeliness of these reports will also give you a sense of the individual's performance.

The information you gather will help you prepare your annual evaluation, but it will also promptly alert you to problems that may be brewing as well as opportunities for coaching and direction on an ongoing basis. Performance reviews may happen only once a year, but the more you prepare, the less you'll need to rush when the time comes.

If you're facing an imminent performance review meeting and you don't have these kinds of records at hand, use the information you do have to jog your memory about your employee's full year of accomplishments. For example, look over your calendar appointments from the past year: You'll be reminded of the week that Tanya impressed you by smoothly covering for her colleagues when half your team was out with the flu, or the time she botched an important presentation during a quarterly division meeting. Similarly, look through your e-mail correspondence and any meeting notes to unearth details that may have been forgotten.

Request an employee self-appraisal

As the performance review date approaches, requesting observations from the employee will also be helpful. Ask your employee to submit a self-appraisal in advance of your review session, explaining that you'll use it to take her point of view into account during your evaluation.

Commissioning a self-appraisal has two major benefits. First, it involves the employee in the review process, which sets a tone of partnership, helps the employee remain open to your feedback, and prepares her for the face-to-face discussion. Second, it gives you another perspective on the employee's work and any potential problems.

Your organization may have a specific self-assessment form for employees to use. If not, you can create one. Anything from a formal written report to a quick list of notes will do. The self-appraisal should address questions such as:

- What are your most important accomplishments and achievements since your last review? Has the past year been better or worse for you than previous years in this position?

- Have you achieved the goals set during your previous review?

- Have you surpassed any of your goals? Which ones? What helped you meet or exceed them?

- Are you struggling with any of your goals? Which ones? What's hindering you from achieving them (poor direction, inadequate resources, lack of training)?

- What do you like most and least about your job?

- What do you hope to achieve in the upcoming year?

- What can your manager or your organization do to better help you succeed?

The sidebar "Theo's self-appraisal" is an example of a document prepared by Theo, a customer service representative. In studying Theo's responses, you can see his side of the story, including what he's struggling with the most, why his goals may or may not have been met, and where he's most likely to focus his attention in the upcoming year.

Solicit 360-degree feedback

While the performance discussion itself will take place just between you and your direct report, you may find it beneficial to supplement your findings with 360-degree feedback, an approach that synthesizes many people's perspectives of the employee's performance.

These collective feedback reports can be time-consuming, and people can be uncomfortable giving their colleagues a formal critical report (even if they complain about their shortcomings behind closed doors). But when done right—in an environment of trust within an organization committed to honest feedback—360s can also provide much more complete information than any single person can.

THEO'S SELF-APPRAISAL

What are your most important accomplishments and achievements since your last review? Has the past year been better or worse for you than previous years in this position?

Learning to use the customer database had the biggest impact on my work this year. Now that I understand the database, I'm able to process twice as many orders per day as I used to. Since I've been here for two years now, I can get many more things done without having to ask questions, so this year has been much better for me than the last.

Have you achieved the goals set during your previous review?

My biggest goal for the year was to improve my processing time for orders, which I've accomplished. Another goal was to improve my knowledge of new product lines, which I was able to do because my mentor instructed me on the new phone script and introduced me to the new products we offer. I also aimed to reduce the number of calls needed to solve customers' problems. I've made progress on this, which I wasn't able to do last year.

Have you surpassed any of your goals? Which ones? What helped you meet or exceed them?

My goal for the year was to increase the orders I process by 25%. I've actually doubled the amount of orders I've processed, thanks to the new customer database. I still have more to learn about the database (the instructional workshop I was supposed to take was cancelled), but fortunately, my colleague Siobhan walked me through the main functions. Siobhan has been a great teacher. Maybe she

(continued)

THEO'S SELF-APPRAISAL

could do a group training on the new database—
I know others are still having problems with it.

Are you struggling with any goals? Which ones?
What's hindering you from achieving them?

One of my goals was to "reduce by 10% the number of calls needed to solve customers' problems." I've been able to reduce the number of calls by 8%. I'm proud of the progress I've made, but I can't do this alone. It might help if someone else on the team were also focusing on call reduction.

What do you like most and least about your job?

I love working with the team and trying new things. But a challenge for me is pacifying angry customers. I get nervous, and they throw me off script. If there's a class or workshop on dealing with difficult customers, I'd be interested in taking it.

What do you hope to achieve in the upcoming year?

I need to continue to learn about new product lines. I'd also like to improve my ability to deal with difficult customers. And while I've made a lot of progress on processing orders faster, I'd like to continue to improve my speed and efficiency.

What can your manager or your organization do to better help you succeed?

Some of my team members are amazing at dealing with difficult customers; a workshop with them could be beneficial. Also, many of the training workshops have been cancelled because of low enrollment. It would help to have these workshops scheduled during weeks that aren't our busiest so that others who are interested could attend.

If an employee's work doesn't bring them into contact with a large variety of people, however, a 360-degree approach may be unnecessary.

To ensure that you gather the most useful information from 360-degree feedback:

- *Clarify your purpose.* Explain to survey respondents and feedback recipients that the purpose of the 360 is to help assess achievements and define areas for improvement, not to amass negative feedback. It should be a constructive process, not a punitive one. Remind respondents, whether they're peers, direct reports, or customers, that if they have ongoing concerns about their working relationship with the employee, they should address those with the individual directly as well.

- *Make your criteria clear.* If you're gathering opinions on hard-to-measure qualities such as "communication skills" or "integrity," ask your respondents for specific examples rather than a numerical rating so you can understand how they've interpreted these qualities. For instance, knowing that a colleague ranked Joe 5 out of 5 in communication tells you (and Joe) much less than "Joe explains project instructions clearly every time. When I have a question, he is happy to sit down with me to make sure we're on the same page for a given assignment."

- *Diversify your pool of respondents.* Ask several peers, direct reports, and internal and external customers to provide input, rather than a few people from one category, or just one person from each category. You'll get a more complete picture, respondents will feel more comfortable responding freely, and the employee being evaluated will know that you've worked to gather a balanced set of data.

Collect additional resources

After you've solicited information from both your direct report and others in the organization, gather any remaining documents that would be helpful in determining whether an employee has improved during the past year. Some of these sources include:

- The most recent job description for the position. In a performance review you're not assessing the quality of your employee—you're evaluating how well this particular person performed a specific job. To identify how well she is doing, you need to first determine what it is you've asked her do.

- The employee's own performance goals and development plan, as defined at her previous review session or earlier in the year. Goals serve as clear benchmarks for success, so these documents will be invaluable in assessing performance. (You'll read more about goals and development plans in the chapter "Establishing Next Steps.")

- The individual's employment records, including past trainings, prior years' evaluation forms, and notes or documentation from previous review sessions.

If you're missing some of these items, you may need to improvise. For example, if your employee's job description is out of date, create a new one. Begin with goals you and your employee have set together, or speak to a human resource manager to compose a current job description to share with the employee.

After you've gathered all the relevant information, you'll need to analyze it and write down your evaluation of the employee. We'll cover both of those topics in the next chapter.

Evaluating Performance

Evaluating Performance

Begin to synthesize your thinking into an overall impression of your employee's performance during the year. Review the information you've gathered, sift through the data you've collected, and make some informal notes. Look for common themes, and give equal consideration to positive results and shortcomings. Has your employee excelled, delivering more than you expected? Has he met your expectations, delivering a solid but not exemplary performance? Or have there been problems, with some goals unmet and results undelivered? It's time to come to a point of view and record it in writing so that you can share it with your employee—and save it for future reference.

Assess results

In theory, assessing the results of your employee's work is simple. Just ask yourself, Has he met the goals set for him since his last review? The easiest achievements to evaluate are those that are quantitative, such as numbers of products shipped, new accounts closed, or reports written. But fewer and fewer jobs today produce easily quantifiable results. To make an objective assessment of your employee's performance on the more qualitative aspects of his job, focus your assessment on his behaviors, using examples for support.

Determine which behaviors are most critical for your employee's successful performance, perhaps by referring back to his job description. For someone in a customer-service position, for example, communication skills are critical, while for a software developer, coding skills are more important. Your organization may also suggest key behaviors or competencies that you'll want to track. For instance, in a company that prizes innovation, creative thinking will be a valuable asset. Beyond the questions that are specific to the position and your company, consider these general attributes suggested by performance management expert Dick Grote:

- *Initiative:* Does the employee demonstrate ambition or take initiative to improve processes and products?

- *Ability to ask questions:* Does the employee know when to ask questions rather than make assumptions?

- *Cooperation and teamwork:* Is the employee flexible when asked to perform a task outside his regular duties or to work extra hours? Does he volunteer to pitch in when the team is short-handed?

- *Communication skills:* Does the employee communicate adequately with managers, peers, and customers? Have any problems been created or solved because of the employee's communication skills?

- *Focus:* Does the employee maintain focus and prioritize job duties effectively?

- *Productivity:* Does the employee work effectively and meet deadlines?

- *Knowledge:* Does the employee demonstrate an acceptable level of knowledge to perform his job?

- *Reliability:* Does the employee consistently demonstrate dependability and competence?

- *Improvement:* Has the employee improved in areas identified as needing development on his previous evaluation?

As you evaluate the employee in each of these areas, look through the materials you've gathered and jot down notes and specific examples. Then consider what factors may have played a role in your direct report's performance. You'll work with him in the discussion itself to sort out many of these root causes (see "Addressing performance gaps" in the next chapter), but in advance of the meeting, assess whether you have contributed to any achievements or performance issues.

Consider your role in the employee's performance

Though it's often difficult to see (or admit), some unsatisfactory performance can be linked to issues with the individual's supervision. Be open to the possibility that your actions or behavior may be a factor in an employee's successes or failures. Honestly assessing how you may have affected an employee can help you evaluate his performance more accurately and fairly.

Some managers, for example, unwittingly erode employees' self-confidence by failing to sufficiently praise good performance or by delivering overly harsh criticism, which diminishes motivation and achievement. Some poor performance can be attributed to a common dynamic that organizational behavior and change management experts Jean-François Manzoni and Jean-Louis Barsoux call the "set-up-to-fail syndrome." In this situation, the manager and direct report start with a positive relationship that gradually worsens because of a poor result—a missed deadline, perhaps, or a lost client. The manager begins to micromanage, and the employee, suspecting his supervisor's reduced confidence, stops doing his best work and avoids making decisions. The manager views this new behavior as additional proof of mediocrity and tightens the screws further, continuing the cycle.

When evaluating areas that are unsatisfactory in your employee's work, consider how you may have contributed to or interfered with an individual's success by asking yourself:

- Have you provided your employee with adequate assistance, training, and resources?

- Have you been clear in your expectations and detailed in your direction?

- Have you set realistic deadlines and established clear priorities?

- Have you tried to motivate the individual to excel?

- Have you been too hands-off, providing insufficient feedback or guidance?

- Have you been too involved, not allowing the individual a chance to succeed independently?

Perhaps, in retrospect, you see that you slowed your employee down by micromanaging, or that he could have made faster progress with more frequent feedback and guidance. Thoughtfully considering your own role in his performance will help you view his work more realistically and make your overall assessment more objective, so you're not assigning blame unnecessarily and you can take the appropriate corrective measures in the future.

Document your impressions

Once you have analyzed your employee's performance, record your feedback in a way that can be shared and saved. When preparing a formal written assessment, refer back to your company's guidelines so you're adhering to the appropriate format. If your company does not have a standard form, create one using Table 1, "Annual performance review template," at the end of this chapter.

Your organization may require you to provide a general rating of the employee's performance, individual ratings of specific aspects of their performance, or a combination of ratings and qualitative information. Follow the instructions given to you, but don't be constrained by the format of the form. Instead, adapt or amend it so you can tell the whole story. Your employee will find your observations, comments, and examples more useful than a numeric rating alone. Include attachments—comments too long to include on the form, or the employee's development plan from the previous year—if they will enrich your evaluation.

Record your observations about your employee's job performance as objectively as possible, and tie your conclusions to hard data. Provide evidence of progress (or lack thereof) by connecting accomplishments with established goals: "Derek increased sales by 7%, which exceeded his goal of 5%." "Laura reduced her error rate by 20%; her goal was 30%." Then your employee can easily grasp the assessment criteria and recognize the evaluation as fair.

Also include specific examples. The more information you can provide, the more likely the employee will be to repeat and even improve on positive behaviors—or correct less positive ones. Use the most telling examples to make your point in your written evaluation, and save the rest for your review session in case you need to support your judgment during the conversation. These examples should include:

- Details about what you observed. Let's look back at Theo, the customer service representative in the previous chapter. Theo has more than doubled the orders he's filled over the past year, now that he's learned how to use the new customer database. But don't just say that; back it up with detail. For example, write: "Last year Theo filled 15 orders per day. This year his average was up to more than 30 per day. He also asks fewer questions now that he's effectively using the customer database."

- Supporting data, such as reports or 360-degree feedback: "Siobhan helped Theo learn how to use the new customer database, and she reports that he's using it on a regular basis."

- The impact on your team and organization: "After Theo learned how to use the new database, he no longer had to rely on colleagues to find out pertinent information. The whole team began fulfilling orders more quickly because they were answering fewer questions from him, which improved cash flow for the organization."

Expressing your observations as neutral facts rather than judgments is particularly important when giving negative feedback. For example, "Theo doesn't seem to care about customers" negatively characterizes Theo rather than describing his behavior. "Theo doesn't know how to talk to difficult customers" also isn't helpful, because it infers a lack of knowledge instead of identifying a skill that Theo can improve upon. On the other hand, "Theo received five complaints from extremely unsatisfied customers," is more objective and specific to a particular job requirement.

When giving positive feedback, on the other hand, combine specific achievements with character-based praise. For example: "With the new accounts she generated, which delivered $1.25 million in business, Juliana exceeded the goal we set for her last July by 27%. Her creativity and perseverance drove her to look beyond the traditional client base; she researched new industries and networked at conferences to find new customers." Acknowledging the traits and behaviors that made those results possible will show your direct report that you see her as an individual—which can generate pride and boost motivation.

Supporting your assessment with specific examples and details not only makes it more likely that the employee will be able to hear and learn from your feedback, it also mitigates any possible legal ramifications in particularly egregious situations. If an employee's work is beginning to suffer, or if you suspect that you might need to dismiss someone due to poor performance, it's vital that you document the individual's behavior and the steps you've taken in attempting to correct it. As a rule of thumb, include in your evaluation only statements that you'd be comfortable testifying to in court. If you have any questions about legal ramifications, consult with your human resource manager or internal legal team.

Finally, write down the three things the employee has done best over the course of the year and the two areas that most need improvement. Ask yourself, "What's the single most important takeaway I want the employee to remember?" Distill your message down to a single key idea—your overall impression of his performance. These few points will determine the overarching message that you want to convey in the review discussion, and having them documented will prevent you from forgetting any important points when you're in the moment.

TABLE 1 *Annual performance review template*

Employee name:

Supervisor:

Employee job title:

Date of review:

Time period being reviewed:
(for example, July 1, 2015–June 30, 2016)

Distillation of job description:
(up to 200 words)

Core individual performance expectations:
(list essential job functions or key job responsibilities)

Organization-wide performance goals:

Departmental performance goals:

MEASURES OF PERFORMANCE

1 = Unsatisfactory: Far below expectations
2 = Fair: Needs improvement
3 = Satisfactory: Meets expectations
4 = Excellent: Exceeds expectations
5 = Exemplary: Greatly exceeds expectations

Achievement of core performance expectations _____
Comments:

Initiative: demonstrates ambition to succeed
in the position; takes initiative to improve
processes and products _____
Comments:

Ability to ask questions: knows when to ask questions
rather than make assumptions _____
Comments:

Cooperation and teamwork: is flexible when asked
to perform a task outside regular duties or to work
extra hours for a special project or pressing deadline _____
Comments:

Communication skills: interacts effectively with
managers, peers, or customers _____
Comments:

Focus: maintains concentration on work to be done;
prioritizes job duties above personal concerns _____
Comments:

(continued)

Productivity: meets productivity requirements and deadlines	_____
Comments:	

Knowledge: demonstrates an acceptable level of knowledge to perform the job	_____
Comments:	

Reliability: consistently demonstrates competence and dependability	_____
Comments:	

Improvement: demonstrates improved performance from previous evaluation	_____
Comments:	

Overall behavior: overall quality of the employee's work _____
Overall impressions:

Strengths:
(no more than three)

Areas for growth and improvement:
(no more than two)

Supervisor signature and date

Employee signature and date

Adapted from Dick Grote, *How to Be Good at Performance Appraisals* (Boston: Harvard Business Review Press, 2011), 98–100.

Conducting
the Meeting

Conducting the Meeting

You've prepared your written evaluation. Now it's time to conduct the meeting. These honest discussions can feel awkward, but if you approach them in the right way, you and your direct report can come out of the session confident and ready to move forward. This chapter will walk you through each step, from preparing for the meeting and setting the right tone once you're in the room to discussing the employee's performance itself.

Prepare for the meeting

Proper handling of logistics can put your employee at ease and smooth the path to an effective review. As you set up the meeting:

- *Schedule it well in advance.* Notify the employee at least a week ahead of the meeting to give both of you plenty of time to prepare.

- *Choose a convenient time.* Don't infringe on personal time by suggesting a meeting during lunch. Set aside 45 to 60 minutes for your conversation, but ensure that neither of you has a pressing commitment immediately afterward in case the discussion takes longer than expected. This will also give your direct report time to work through any emotions brought on by a difficult conversation.

- *Select a neutral location.* Find a spot that's private and free from distractions and interruptions. You'll both be most comfortable in a business setting—your office, an empty office, or a conference room—rather than in a public environment, such as a cafeteria or coffee shop. If you do meet in your office, sit beside your employee to establish a sense of partnership and open communication. Sitting behind your desk can convey dominance and distance.

- *Agree on content.* Discuss the nature of the meeting with the employee ahead of time, even if the two of you have had review sessions in the past. Tell her what you plan to discuss during the meeting, such as her self-appraisal, your completed evaluation, a summary of her strengths, and a discussion about areas for improvement.

Keep in mind that some employees may require special arrangements regarding schedule, meeting location, and content if the discussion has the possibility of escalating to an uncomfortable level. (See the section "Addressing unacceptable performance" in the final chapter of this book.)

To support your conversation, gather all of the relevant materials you've referenced throughout the appraisal process thus far. Make sure your direct report feels equally prepared: Give her a copy of your assessment to read an hour or two before the meeting, and ask that she jot down any reactions or questions she wants to discuss. This allows her the privacy to react emotionally and begin digesting the information, so she'll be more composed and ready for a productive discussion.

Set the right tone

Most people, even the highest of achievers, approach performance review meetings with some sense of dread. Anticipating a manager's criticism, no matter how constructive or well meaning, can make an employee understandably anxious. And many managers feel awkward delivering such feedback, wondering if the employee will become defensive or upset.

To mitigate anxiety on your or your employee's part, set a tone of partnership right from the start. Establish a rapport by welcoming your employee. Limit distractions: Silence your cell phone, and if you're near your computer, turn off any audible notifications.

Remind your direct report that the purpose of the review is to determine how the individual can best meet her goals and to help you understand what she needs to excel in her job. Tell her explicitly that her input is necessary and valuable, and that you hope the conversation will be an open dialogue, so you can work together as partners on any issues that arise. You should also let your employee know that you'd like to take notes so that you can both remember what you've discussed (see the sidebar "Taking notes").

TAKING NOTES

During your discussion, document key points and outcomes. Doing so is good for both of you: In case you later disagree about what was discussed or planned during the review session (or in the rarer case of a legal dispute), you can check the record.

Include the following elements in your notes:

- The date of the meeting

- Names of attendees (in some instances, your boss or human resource representative may attend)

- Key points and phrases used during the meeting

- Any points of disagreement

If you discuss any plans or objectives moving forward (covered in the next chapter), also include:

- Performance goals for the coming year

- An overview of any development plans you and your direct report discuss

- A summary of agreed-upon next steps

Even if you're an inveterate computer user, take notes with pen and paper; a computer screen can create distance between you and your direct report. Type up your notes right after the meeting, while your memory is still fresh.

Your organization may require you to distribute copies of this record to the employee and to HR for the employee's file, in addition to keeping a copy for yourself. Some organizations require that both manager and employee sign the performance review report, and sometimes the employee has the right to append her own comments.

After stating the purpose and objectives of the meeting, ask the employee to talk about her self-appraisal. This will help you understand her perspective on her performance and prevent you from controlling too much of the conversation early on. If she's hesitant to speak up, ask probing questions to get her started: "How do you feel things are going on the job? What's going well, and what problems are you having?" This is the time to focus on her point of view, not to agree or disagree on specific points.

During the conversation, practice active listening. Don't interrupt. Show that you're paying close attention by periodically paraphrasing what you've heard after your employee has finished talking. For example, "If I understand you correctly, you feel that you are meeting all goals with respect to the weekly sales reports, but that you are struggling to contact all the key customers you've been assigned. Do I have that right?" This gives your employee the opportunity to correct any misunderstandings.

Discuss employee performance

During your performance review session, you might feel nervous—or even reluctant—to offer constructive feedback. But even your most stellar employees can benefit from ideas for improvement—and if you don't take this opportunity to deliver them, your time-consuming evaluation won't have much use.

Frame your feedback as a way to reach a goal-related outcome, such as boosting sales or improving service. It then becomes an opportunity to solve a business problem rather than a time to criticize a person. Or focus on the employee's development—the feedback then becomes an investment in her career. Throughout your discussion, make your employee's performance the subject of the conversation, rather than the employee herself. As in your written evaluation, don't say anything negative that could be perceived as a statement about her character, values, or intentions (such as, "You don't seem dedicated to this project"). A character attack offers no ideas for change and puts your employee on the defensive, which makes learning nearly impossible. Instead, use straightforward, neutral language, such as, "I've noticed that you haven't offered any suggestions at our service improvement meetings. Why is that?" Even with employees who need to improve their performance significantly, take care not to express any anger, judgment, or contempt.

Don't rely on your written assessment to dictate the agenda of your meeting. Doing so can lock you and the employee into an item-by-item negotiation rather than a productive discussion. Instead, use your evaluation as a reference so you don't forget important points in the conversation.

Base the appraisal discussion on how previously agreed-upon performance goals relate to specific business outcomes. For example, you might say, "We agreed that you would bring in 10 new clients this quarter, and you exceeded that goal," or "We agreed that you'd reduce the number of production line errors by 10%, but you've only reduced them by 5." Home in on issues that the employee can improve in the future. Be selective; you don't need to recite every shortcoming or failing you've noticed.

Recognizing strong performance

For those employees whose results and behaviors fully meet or exceed expectations, concentrate on their strengths by identifying and celebrating their successes. Thank your employee for her contributions. She may not know how much you appreciate her good work. This will grab her attention and also reduce the defensiveness that she might have felt going into the performance review.

Move on to discuss specific examples you've listed in your evaluation where her successes and strengths were most apparent: "You've increased sales by 8%, you did a terrific job organizing the quarterly sales meetings, and your contributions at staff meetings are exemplary." By starting with her most important contributions and most noteworthy strengths, focusing on achievements, and pinpointing the behaviors that led to success, you'll encourage your employee to feel motivated and energized.

For these star performers, introduce improvements within the context of their strengths and contributions. Your conscientious employee will likely herself acknowledge missed targets or unmet goals and may initiate a discussion of opportunities for improvement. If so, she can take the lead in discussing improvement—which may make her more invested in the conversation and more motivated to improve.

If your direct report doesn't volunteer any areas for improvement, prompt her to do so. You might ask questions such as: How do you see the situation? What do you think worked, and what could have gone better? How might you do things differently in the future? By asking questions, rather than making statements, you can establish a supportive atmosphere without devaluing any of her accomplishments. By answering your questions, the employee can raise issues and explore alternative approaches. This will afford her more control of the conversation and a sense of ownership of the improvements she suggests.

Addressing performance gaps

For those direct reports who require corrective feedback, you'll need to clearly define where performance gaps exist. Which of their goals went unmet? You'll still want to lead with the positive, however. To start, note any areas in which your employee did meet or exceed her goals. Acknowledging achievements first will establish trust and goodwill by showing that your evaluation is fair and based on previously agreed-upon criteria. This will also make your employee more receptive to your recommendations for improvement. That being said, don't sugarcoat bad news by sandwiching it between positive points, as that can confuse your message (see the sidebar "Beware the sandwich approach").

Once you've highlighted your direct report's accomplishments, describe the gap between the goal in

BEWARE THE SANDWICH APPROACH

For no employee should you use the shopworn "sandwich" approach, in which you name a few strengths, then some weaknesses, and then more compliments. The problem with this seemingly balanced method is that it lacks a single clear, consistent message. With the sandwich approach, you risk demoralizing your stars, who will fixate on the negatives, and falsely encouraging marginal performers, who may tune into praise without registering criticism.

Instead, concentrate your conversation on either celebrating success or triggering change—but not both.

question and the actual performance: "We were aiming for ten new accounts by the end of the quarter, and we closed seven." Don't compound the trouble of performance gaps by assigning blame; instead, work with your employee to uncover the root causes. Ask for the individual's input: "Why do you think your sales this year have fallen short of your goal?" Give your employee the first opportunity to identify the cause, and listen carefully.

The reasons for poor performance may not always be obvious and may have nothing to do with skill or motivation. It may be the result of flawed work processes, personal problems, conflicts with coworkers, or even exhaustion or burnout. Talking together to uncover the reasons for performance gaps will, in most cases, create an atmosphere of objectivity in which both you and your direct report can contribute in positive ways.

If your employee doesn't independently identify her stumbling blocks, ask more questions: Does she need more product information or training? Are there too many distractions in the office? Does she have sufficient resources at hand to get the job done? Is the scope of her responsibilities clear? Your questions and statements will come across as attempts to problem solve, rather than to attack, so your employee will be less likely to react defensively. And you might discover that the gap between desired performance and actual results was really caused by a different sort of problem, such as unrealistic deadlines or unclear expectations.

Once you've teased out the causes behind any performance shortfalls, you're armed with the material you need to create an action plan with your employee, which should happen at a separate meeting. Before your review session ends, take a moment to summarize what you've discussed and suggest a way to move forward: "Let's think about the things we've discussed today and meet next week to develop our course of action." We'll explain how to do that in the next chapter.

Establishing Next Steps

Establishing Next Steps

A performance review discussion is the natural end of an appraisal cycle—and the beginning of a new one. After the meeting is over, hold a separate performance-planning session with your direct report to identify goals and create a development plan for the next year.

Allowing some time between the two meetings will give your employee the opportunity to process the conversation, digest your feedback, and gather information needed to create a meaningful plan for development. A week between the two meetings is ideal, but even a few days is helpful.

Set goals

Meaningful goals will provide motivation and direction and help your employee understand how to invest his time, energy, and resources. Goals define the results an employee will aim to achieve over the next year, making them a valuable mechanism for providing ongoing and year-end feedback.

Suitable goals will come from different sources for different people. Performance gaps and comments noted during the previous review period may be an obvious source of goals for some employees. For high achievers with minor performance gaps, think beyond their work results to their career ambitions. What objectives could such an individual pursue to expand her role or increase her contribution to the organization? (See the sidebar "Career development.") If your organization or field is in a rapid state of change, or if an individual is on a fast track to success and mastery, goals may change drastically from one year to the next.

Other sources for goals may include an employee's job description or your department's or organization's plans and strategies. Consider which parts of the individual's job are most time consuming and which aspects have the biggest impact on departmental or organizational success. How can more time and focus be spent on those assignments that matter most?

Give your direct report the opportunity to participate as much as possible in developing his own goals. When your employee has input into setting these objectives, he will feel a valuable sense of ownership— and people are naturally more committed to things they own. They also feel more engaged if they understand how their work contributes to big-picture success, so connect each employee's goals to larger organizational and unit ambitions, articulating how an individual's efforts support the larger strategy.

CAREER DEVELOPMENT

If your employees aren't growing or developing, they may grow bored and unmotivated—which means you're at risk of having them leave for more interesting, challenging work elsewhere. A well-thought-out plan for employees' skill and career development can boost morale and motivation, enriching their work experience so they continue to build skills and make valuable contributions. As a manager, your role is to help them determine how to keep improving.

Keep in mind that your employees—especially your top performers—may have their own set of career ambitions they'd like to pursue in the coming year. Creating a development plan for an employee requires that you have an understanding of those aspirations as well as his current skill set, motivation, and values. Engage him in a conversation, asking questions such as "What do you want to be known for?" or "What matters most to you in your work?" This will give your employee a chance to reflect on his career path. When you understand what he wants from his career, you can figure out ways to broaden his professional experience and align his aspirations with the larger interests of the organization.

Don't allow good people to get stuck on career plateaus. For individuals with the talent and motivation to move toward a higher-level role—someone you'll want to promote in the future—identify any gaps between the skills and experience they have now and those they'll need for a higher position.

As you define goals with your direct reports:

- *Make their goals challenging.* At their best, goals should be achievable but ambitious. The toughest targets usually spur the greatest levels of effort and performance, energizing people to meet a challenge. But make sure that any demanding goals are not impossible. Overly ambitious goals can backfire; if an employee can't possibly meet an objective, he may feel frustrated or unmotivated, and may ignore the goal entirely. Targets that can be reached too easily, however, can result in low effort and mediocre work. It can be helpful to set tough goals as a range ("increase sales between 15%–20%") rather than a narrow benchmark ("bring in $2 million in new business"). Flexible expectations allow for psychological breathing room.

    People are more likely to pursue challenging objectives when they see a personal benefit.

Discuss what achievement of a tough goal may bring: greater visibility in the organization, skill development (which can lead to promotion), recognition, or even a financial bonus, if that's customary in your organization.

- *Make their goals measurable.* How will you know if a target has been met? As we've seen, for goals that can be measured quantitatively— such as sales revenue, number of errors, or time to market—assessing achievement is a simple matter of looking at the numbers. More qualitative goals, such as those related to professional development or customer satisfaction, are harder to measure. We know that one way around this is to analyze the employee's behaviors, but you can also set goals to measure the more tangible facets of a qualitative skill. For example, there's no obvious measure of "customer relations," but you may be able to quantify the average time needed to resolve a customer's problem or the number of customer complaints handled satisfactorily per quarter. Determine in advance how you plan to measure progress toward each objective.

- *Don't set too many goals.* When you establish too many objectives for your employee, the importance of each one may become trivial and the individual is likely to make less progress on each one. Limit the number of goals for your employee to three or four. The smaller the number, the more important each one will be.

Keep in mind that the goals you formally instate are just one part of the employee's job—they are not the whole job. Many important aspects of performance— such as helping a colleague in a last-minute crunch, or coaching a new member of the team—aren't suitable targets for goal setting.

Create a development plan

A development plan specifies how an employee will reach his goals. How can your direct report eliminate any performance issues you've discussed while also reaching those agreed-upon objectives? Begin by asking him what he would propose. As with the goal-setting process, giving the employee the first opportunity to suggest a plan can increase his sense of ownership of the solution—and make him feel more committed to following through. Offer ideas to strengthen the plan, and challenge any questionable assumptions.

Rarely is there only one solution to a problem, so if your employee is having trouble putting together a credible plan, discuss a few different approaches. Offering flexible options in resolving a problem demonstrates that the choice is about how—not if—a problem will be fixed. You can suggest solutions such as training or coaching, on-the-job practice, or working closely with a more skilled associate.

Once you decide which steps to take, document them. (Use Table 2, "Individual development plan template," at the end of this chapter as a sample form to get you started if your company hasn't provided one for you.)

First, list each of the goals that you and your direct report have agreed upon. Include next to each of those goals any details on how they'll be measured or what you expect outcomes to look like.

Then, for each performance goal, describe specific actions that your employee will take to fulfill each one:

- Break down each goal into isolated tasks, with interim objectives and clear outcomes.

- Plan the execution of those tasks and assign start and end dates.

- Establish clear checkpoints for progress; set milestones, perhaps monthly or quarterly, along the way to monitor progress toward the goal.

- Determine the resources needed to fulfill each task, such as time, equipment, training or coaching, or assistance from support staff. Make sure sufficient resources are allotted to fulfill each task.

- Discuss any contingency plans. What will happen if something goes wrong while the employee is working toward the goal? What are possible risks, and how could he manage them?

Keep a copy of the development plan, and give a copy to your direct report. Seeing a written record of next steps and commitments can keep targets foremost in mind. With a clear set of goals and a logical plan, your employee will know what you expect of him and how he'll be evaluated, and you'll have a practical guide to assessing his performance over the course of the year and preparing for next year's review.

Monitor progress and follow up

Your task isn't over, however. As a manager, you'll need to continue to check on progress, provide feedback, and determine whether your direct report needs additional training, coaching, or support throughout the year. Frequent feedback and interaction will help your direct report meet goals and stay on track.

Arrange weekly or biweekly meetings with your employee to discuss his progress, or consider scheduling follow-ups according to the deadlines and key dates documented in his development plan. Your goal in these meetings is to understand your employee's progress against this plan. You'll find that check-ins provide an opportunity to reinforce learning, prevent backsliding, and continue improvement. Frequent follow-up sessions allow for early intervention if an employee isn't meeting the mark. They also provide an opportunity to recognize and reinforce good work and to celebrate when your direct report achieves a goal.

If an individual isn't used to hearing feedback often, he may initially be startled or even bristle at this ongoing dialogue. But monitoring and meeting with your employee on a regular basis will, over time, make the process easier and more familiar. Frequent feedback can help both of you establish a partnership in achieving goals and start a real dialogue about how the employee can grow and develop.

In these meetings, ask your employee what's going well and what isn't. Is he on track to meet his goals? Encourage him to note his achievements, identify needed resources, and pinpoint factors that support or hinder his work. In addition, make it clear that you hold yourself accountable in supporting his success. You might ask how you can continue to support his progress or how the organization can better help him achieve his goals.

Few people meet every goal without encountering some bumps in the road. When things are going well for your employee, acknowledge that success. But if an individual encounters obstacles in achieving a goal and the contingency plan you agreed upon doesn't seem to be working, ask him to suggest a potential solution. If that doesn't work, get more involved through activities such as coaching. Your direct report's goals and development plans may need to be modified if he continues to struggle. But even if goals or plans change, taking an active role in helping your employee meet his goals will help him feel supported and understood.

Monitor an employee with significant performance gaps particularly carefully; meet with him often to stay on top of his progress and challenges. If he doesn't make progress or meaningful contributions, his employment may be at risk; the more often you check his progress, the more you'll be able to gauge his status.

Feedback and follow-up should not be restricted to struggling employees, however. It's essential that you give feedback to all employees, whether they are strong performers who independently raise concerns or poor performers with specific problem areas.

Evaluate your approach

Effectively reviewing employees' performance takes practice, so assess your own performance as you monitor your employee's progress, and consider how you might make improvements. After the goal-setting meeting, ask for feedback: How did the review process go? What was useful, and what was not? For instance, perhaps you didn't provide enough specific examples of performance gaps or give the employee enough time to complete his self-appraisal. Ask for suggestions for ways to do things differently in the future. You'll build trust when an individual sees you acting on the things he mentions.

Also think about how you handled the preparation process and the conversation itself. Did you create an open climate for communication? Did you listen carefully to what the employee said? Was your feedback clear and specific? What worked well, and what could be improved next time?

Compare your view with any feedback your employee offered, and determine what changes you can make for future reviews. Conducting a performance review isn't easy, but with practice and thoughtful reflection, you can become more effective and comfortable.

By now you understand all the elements of the performance review process. Next, you'll learn how to manage particular kinds of difficult conversations that may arise during your discussion.

TABLE 2 *Individual development plan template*

List three primary goals the individual will accomplish in the upcoming year. Include a description of how those goals will be measured and/or the expected outcomes.

Goals	Measures of achievement/expected outcomes
1.	
2.	
3.	

Describe specific tasks that need to be completed to accomplish each of the three goals above and assign a start and an end date for each. Include a plan for executing the tasks, checkpoints for progress, resources needed, and possible contingency plans.

GOAL 1:

Tasks required:	Start date:	End date:

Plan for executing the tasks:

(continued)

Checkpoints for progress:

_____

Resources needed:

_____

Contingency plans:

_____

GOAL 2:

_____

Tasks required: Start date: End date:

_____

_____

_____

Plan for executing the tasks:

_____

Checkpoints for progress:

_____

Resources needed:

_____

Contingency plans:

_____

GOAL 3:

Tasks required:	Start date:	End date:

Plan for executing the tasks:

Checkpoints for progress:

Resources needed:

Contingency plans:

Include any additional notes about the development plan here:

THIS PLAN IS AGREED TO AS INDICATED BY THE SIGNATURES BELOW.

Employee	Date
Manager	Date

Handling Tough Topics

Handling Tough Topics

No matter how well you prepare, you may run into some difficult situations as you hold your performance review discussion. This chapter will cover tough topics that you may need to discuss, such as raises, promotions, or particularly poor performance.

Responding to a raise request

Many employees use their performance review meeting to ask for a raise. If possible, keep this discussion separate by holding it at a later date. Performance and compensation are each significant enough on their own, and it's usually not ideal to mix the two. Thank the person for bringing up the request, and promise to get back to her by a specific date. (If it's already been decided whether a raise will be granted, however, and the individual is set on discussing it as part of your review meeting, do so at the beginning of your conversation; otherwise your employee may be too distracted to listen to your feedback.)

If a decision has not yet been made, you will need time to fairly assess the situation and decide whether an increase in pay is appropriate. When you do meet to discuss the request, explain that an individual's salary is determined by two factors: the value of the job itself to the organization and the quality of the individual's performance. Regardless of the individual in the role, every job holds a certain market value. If that position's pay isn't negotiable because it has reached the peak compensation allowed by the company for that role, rejecting a raise request will clearly reflect only the value of the job to the organization, not on the person's worth as an individual.

Ask the employee to consider both factors, examining both how the job can be made more valuable to the organization and how her performance can be improved. What additional duties could she take on? How much extra responsibility could she assume? Discuss these possibilities in light of the performance review discussion you've conducted. Once these issues have been settled, follow your organization's procedure for determining if a raise is warranted or possible.

Discussing a promotion

An employee might also use the review session to request a promotion—an elevation in title as well as in salary. As a manager, you might feel responsible for helping others move up in an organization, but promotion decisions require careful consideration. As with a raise request, don't respond immediately. You need time to determine if the individual is truly ready for the next challenge.

Rewarding an individual with a promotion sends a signal to the rest of your organization, so only endorse behavior that reflects organizational values. For example, in a workplace that values teamwork, someone who meets all her sales targets but mistreats team members would not be a wise candidate for a promotion.

Keep in mind, also, that a traditional move up the career ladder—taking on more management responsibilities—isn't the right path for all employees. An operations genius might not find the "reward" of a higher-level managerial position appealing. Is the new job a fit with her interests and skills? Would she enjoy the position? Ask the employee if she's excited about the potential new responsibilities. If not, consider a more flexible path to success, such as an alternative role that meets an organizational need while also fulfilling her ambitions.

Before moving forward with a promotion, be certain that the individual will be able to do the job she has asked for. Having just reviewed her performance will make it easier to assess her on this front, as her current performance will likely illustrate how she'll do in the new role. You may also consider gathering others' input (if you didn't already use 360-degree feedback during your evaluation process). You may discover that your employee is already successfully taking on tasks that are part of the new position— which is the best evidence that she's ready to move up.

If your direct report's performance in her current position isn't a useful predictor of success in the new role, you'll probably need more information before you move her into a new permanent position. Before making a final decision, create an assignment similar to a task she'd take on if promoted. This will allow you to assess how well she'll perform in the new role. Outline criteria for success in the assignment, and establish a (short) timeline for evaluation. Make it clear that this is a short-term assignment, not an ongoing responsibility. (If you change the scope of her position without a corresponding change of title or pay, she may become dissatisfied or frustrated.)

If you determine that an individual is not, in fact, ready for a promotion, discuss your concerns with her and provide a clear explanation as to why you're declining her request. Discuss which tasks and assignments can best prepare her for the next step. Then create an action plan to address how she can develop the skills and experiences she will need to move up. You might formalize this course of action in her development plan.

Of course, as you decide whether an individual is ready for promotion, always follow your organization's guidelines, processes, and requirements.

Addressing unacceptable performance

Often teams are made up of a mix of high achievers, those who simply meet expectations, and those who still require improvement in certain areas. But, more rarely, you will encounter a subpar performer who needs stark, critical feedback in her performance review—as well as immediate improvement on her part—to continue employment with the organization.

If an employee's performance—either her work results, behaviors, or a combination of both—is poor, the focus of the review session should be on an immediate turnaround. Planning for this conversation will be different than it would for better-performing employees.

Do not give marginal performers a copy of your appraisal for review in advance of the meeting, and, if possible, don't have the employee fill out a self-appraisal. Such tasks can reinforce the mistaken perception that all is well, and your task is to make the individual realize that, in truth, it is not.

Hold the meeting in your office. Unlike in review sessions with solid or good performers, where you worked to establish equal footing, it's appropriate in this situation to sit in a position of authority, behind your desk with the employee in front of you. If possible, schedule the meeting for the end of the day. The individual may have a strong reaction, and it will be easier for her to leave the office afterward than to return to her desk and pretend everything is fine.

As with solid and successful performers, open your conversation by reminding the employee of the purpose of the review and acknowledging that this sort of meeting can feel awkward. Then get right to the point: "I need to tell you that your performance is not acceptable. I want to spend our time together talking about the problems I see. Then I'd like to hear your ideas about what you can do to correct this situation."

After this opening, explain what problems you perceive—and make it clear that these problems must be solved. The following steps can be useful:

- State your concern precisely: "Your approach to customer service is of serious concern."

- Follow with examples: "Customers have complained about your sarcastic and condescending tone. They've reported that you've called their questions 'dumb' or 'obvious,' and a few have escalated to the point of needing management's involvement."

- Close by requesting the employee's reaction to your perception, and make a specific mandate for change: "We need to decide how to proceed so that your work is a better fit for the objectives of this company and our customers, or we may need to explore whether customer service is the right career for you."

Hopefully the ongoing feedback you have been giving this employee will make this assessment less of a surprise, but chances are that direct confrontation about the employee's unacceptable performance will be painful for her to hear. Like most employees, a marginal performer is probably used to the old sandwich-technique review, which enabled her to selectively focus on the few positive comments she received and brush off any discussion of problems. She may be surprised that you are focusing directly on her unacceptable performance and may respond with what she sees as her accomplishments. Or she may argue that previous reviews have always been positive and that her work this year has been no different. Acknowledge that the employee may not have had the facts presented clearly in previous discussions, and reemphasize that her performance this year was not at an acceptable level. Make it clear that she will need to correct the situation immediately if she is to remain employed.

As a manager, you may well find this approach uncomfortable. But excessive diplomacy can be just as damaging as undue harshness. Avoiding offense will only muddy your message and create less-effective feedback. Employees can't adjust their behavior in a meaningful way if you give them indirect, sugar-coated criticism. Embrace the opportunity to deliver meaningful criticism: Every employee deserves an honest assessment.

Some poor performers, however, honestly believe their work has been satisfactory. In this case, correct the misconception by discussing specific examples you've noted in your evaluation, and give the employee an opportunity to improve. The individual's performance may get substantially better with direction, support, follow-up, and regular feedback.

For some employees, no amount of coaching, training, or feedback can coax performance to an acceptable level. The performance review or ensuing plans to correct performance gaps may have confirmed that the employee's performance is beyond your organization's resources to change. If the employee and organization are irredeemably mismatched, termination may be the right course of action, at which point you should speak to your HR department and follow your organization's guidelines for dismissing the employee.

Whether your direct report is struggling or soaring, the performance review process includes many important and sometimes difficult tasks—from gathering the right information, evaluating performance, and conducting potentially awkward conversations to creating realistic development plans and following up in a disciplined way. But by actively pursuing some of these activities—such as collecting your observations and giving regular feedback—throughout the year, you'll help ensure that the next appraisal period is less stressful and more effective. Done right, performance reviews can be among your best assets in cultivating great performance in each of your employees, your team, and your organization.

Learn More

Quick hits

Dattner, Ben. "In Performance Appraisals, Make Context Count." HBR.org, June 3, 2013. http://hbr.org/2013/06/in-performance-appraisals-make/.

An individual's performance is difficult to measure. Organizational psychologist Ben Dattner argues that organizations could achieve greater accuracy in performance evaluations by considering both the person *and* the situation in which his performance is being assessed. In this piece, readers will learn how looking at the broader situation can lead to a fairer and less biased appraisal and what questions to ask to include these considerations in their assessments.

"Goal Setting: The Art of Stretch Goals." HBR.org Video, February 15, 2011. http://hbr.org/2011/02/goal-setting-the-art-of-stretc/.

Setting challenging goals, also known as stretch targets, can energize your employee, encourage her to think more creatively about how to achieve certain objectives, and help create a high-performance culture. But if those goals are *too* challenging, they can weaken morale. In this video, Srikant Datar, board member at Novartis, discusses the delicate balance between goals that are motivating and those that are simply discouraging.

Sytch, Maxim and D. Scott DeRue. "Ditch Performance Reviews? How About Learn to Do Them Well?" HBR.org, June 22, 2010. http://hbr.org/2010/06/ditch-performance -reviews-how/.

Many managers balk at the idea of doing performance appraisals, claiming they're ineffective. But research reveals that these evaluations can lead to improved performance. In this piece, the authors explain three challenges that prevent performance reviews from being effective—and provide four tips managers should remember to do them well.

Books

Falcone, Paul. *2600 Phrases for Effective Performance Reviews*. New York: AMACOM, 2005.

Struggling to find the right words to describe a direct report's performance? In this book, Falcone provides a variety of phrases to assist managers in writing performance appraisals and communicating feedback effectively. Whether searching by core competency or by job function, readers can find the right words to express their thoughts in a concrete manner.

Green, Marnie E. *Painless Performance Conversations: A Practical Approach to Critical Day-to-Day Workplace Discussions.* Hoboken, NJ: Wiley, 2013.

Green helps managers conquer their anxieties about performance appraisals, allowing them to have effective feedback conversations with their direct reports, whether it's in day-to-day interactions or an annual performance review meeting. Her book provides summary tips, reflection questions, conversation checkpoints, and case studies to help managers stop dwelling on their discomfort and start focusing on improving performance.

Grote, Dick. *How to Be Good at Performance Appraisals: Simple, Effective, Done Right.* Boston: Harvard Business Review Press, 2011.

This hands-on guide goes beyond the scope of this 20-Minute Manager to explain how to succeed at every task required by a company's performance appraisal and management process. Using step-by-step instructions, examples, sample dialogues, and suggested scripts, performance management expert Grote shows the reader how to handle appraisal activities ranging from setting goals, defining job responsibilities, and coaching to assessing performance, conducting the discussion, and creating development plans.

Harvard Business School Publishing. *HBR Guide to Giving Effective Feedback*. Boston: Harvard Business Review Press, 2012.

Productive performance discussions start with effective feedback. Filled with actionable advice on everything from delivering on-the-spot feedback to determining whether an employee is ready for a promotion, this guide offers tools for giving positive and constructive feedback. Readers will learn how to incorporate feedback into daily interactions with employees, reward direct reports with greater compensation and responsibility, reinforce organizational values and goals, and deliver constructive criticism without generating anger or defensiveness.

Articles

Hattersley, Michael E. "How to Get the Best Out of Performance Reviews." *Harvard Management Communication Letter*, May 1999 (product #C9905A).

Not all workers perform equally well. How do you deal with both the good and the bad effectively? This article provides illustrative examples to help managers improve their performance appraisal skills when handling a poor performer, coping with an average worker, and recognizing excellence.

Kindall, Alva F., and James Gatza. "Positive Program for Performance Appraisal." *Harvard Business Review*, November–December 1963 (product #63609).

Despite their best efforts, many managers discover that their company's performance appraisal processes are flawed. One solution is to give an employee a stronger voice in discussing her performance and goals. In this classic HBR article, the authors describe how to create a "target-setting appraisal," which starts with the direct report, not the manager.

Peiperl, Maury A. "Getting 360-Degree Feedback Right." *Harvard Business Review*, January–February 2001 (product #R0101K).

Under what circumstances does peer appraisal improve performance? Why does 360-degree feedback sometimes work well and sometimes fail? And how can executives make these programs less anxiety provoking for participants and more productive for organizations? For years, Peiperl has studied 360-degree feedback with these questions in mind. In this article, he identifies the four inescapable paradoxes of 360-feedback and explains how to manage them.

Sources

Ashkenas, Ron. "Firing Someone the Right Way." HBR.org, March 20, 2012. http://hbr.org/2012/03/firing-someone -the-right-way/.

Ballaro, Beverly. "Making Performance Reviews Less Stressful—for Everyone." *Harvard Management Update*, January 2008 (product #U0801A).

Beer, Michael. "Conducting a Performance Appraisal Interview." Case note. Boston: Harvard Business School, 1997 (product #497058).

Gabarro, John J., and Linda A. Hill. "Managing Performance." Case note. Boston: Harvard Business School, 1996 (product #496022).

Grote, Dick. *How to Be Good at Performance Appraisals: Simple, Effective, Done Right*. Boston: Harvard Business Review Press, 2011.

Grote, Dick. "How to Handle a Raise Request." HBR.org, June 20, 2011. http://hbr.org/2011/06/how-to-deal-with -a-raise-reque/.

Grote, Dick. "Making the Performance Appraisal System Work." In *The Complete Guide to Performance Appraisal*. New York: AMACOM, 1996.

Harvard Business School Publishing. *Harvard Business Essentials: Manager's Toolkit*. Boston: Harvard Business School Publishing, 2004.

Harvard Business School Publishing. *Harvard Business Essentials: Performance Management*. Boston: Harvard Business School Publishing, 2006.

Harvard Business School Publishing. *HBR Guide to Giving Effective Feedback*. Boston: Harvard Business Review Press, 2012.

Harvard Business School Publishing. *Performance Appraisal*. Boston: Harvard Business Press, 2009.

Harvard Business School Publishing. *Setting Goals*. Boston: Harvard Business Press, 2009.

Johnson, Lauren Keller. "The Ratings Game: Retooling 360s for Better Performance." *Harvard Management Update*, January 2004 (product #U0401A).

Knight, Rebecca. "Delivering an Effective Performance Review." HBR.org, November 3, 2011. http://hbr.org/2011/11/delivering-an-effective-perfor/.

Manzoni, Jean-François and Jean-Louis Barsoux. "The Set-Up-to-Fail Syndrome." *Harvard Business Review*, March 1998 (product #98209).

Prewitt, Edward. "Should You Use 360-Degree Feedback for Performance Reviews?" *Harvard Management Update*, February 1999 (product #U9902C).

Sytch, Maxim and D. Scott DeRue. "Ditch Performance Reviews? How About Learn to Do Them Well?" HBR.org, June 22, 2010. http://hbr.org/2010/06/ditch-performance-reviews-how/.

Index

Notes

Smarter than the average guide.

Harvard Business Review Guides

If you enjoyed this book and want more comprehensive guidance on essential professional skills, turn to the **HBR Guides series**. Packed with concise, practical tips from leading experts—and examples that make them easy to apply—these books help you master big work challenges with advice from the most trusted brand in business.

 **Harvard Business Review** Press

AVAILABLE IN PAPERBACK
OR EBOOK FORMAT
WHEREVER BOOKS ARE SOLD

- Better Business Writing
- Coaching Employees
- Finance Basics for Managers
- Getting the Mentoring You Need
- Getting the Right Work Done

- Managing Stress at Work
- Managing Up and Across
- Office Politics
- Persuasive Presentations
- Project Management